HIT THE WALL

Ike Holter

BROADWAY PLAY PUBLISHING INC
New York
www.broadwayplaypub.com
info@broadwayplaypub.com

First edition: June 2019
I S B N: 978-0-88145-845-9

Book design: Marie Donovan
Page make-up: Adobe InDesign
Typeface: Palatino

The world premiere of HIT THE WALL was presented on 3 February 2012 by The Inconvenience and performed as part of Garage Rep: three productions presented in rotating repertory in The Garage at Steppenwolf in Chicago (Chris Chmelik, Artistic Director and Missi Davis, Executive Director). The cast and creative contributors were as follows:

A-GAY	Layne Manzer
NEWBIE	Daniel Desmaris
CARSON	Manny Buckley
PEG	Rania Salem Manganaro
CLIFF	Steve Lenz
ROBERTA	Shannon Matesky
TANO	Arturo Soria
MIKA	Desmond Gray
COP	Walter Owen Briggs
MADELINE	Mary Williamston

Director	Eric Hoff
Choreographer	Erin Kilmurray
Original music	Ryan Murphy
Music direction	John Cicora
Scenic design	John Holt
Costume design	Coral Gable
Lighting design	Jeff Glass
Sound design	Joe Court

HIT THE WALL was originally produced Off-Broadway by the Barrow Street Theatre on 10 March 2013. The cast and creative contributors were as follows:

A-GAY ....Sean Allan Krill
NEWBIE.. Nick Bailey
CARSON ....Nathan Lee Graham
PEG... Rania Salem Manganaro
CLIFF .... Ben Diskant
ROBERTA ....Carolyn Michelle Smith
TANO ....Arturo Soria
MIKA... Gregory Haney
COP ....Matthew Greer
MADELINE ....Jessica Dickey

Director...Eric Hoff
Original music & music supervision .... Dan Lipton,
Music direction .... Jonathan Mastro
Fight direction...J David Brimmer
Scenic design... Lauren Helpern
Costume design.. David Hyman
Lighting design .... Keith Parham
Sound design................Daniel Kluger & Brandon Wolcott
Production stage manager .... Bethany Russell

CHARACTERS

A-GAY, *late 20s, early 30s. Attractive, smooth talking Harvard Grad who can pass for straight. A clipped, uncaring vampire with a great closing argument.*

NEWBIE, *fresh off the boat early twenties queer. Not only knows where the party is; he leads it.*

CARSON, *black, strong and silent type with a hidden cache of bitchisims that could clear a room. Sticks to his morals till they're pried from his fingers.*

PEG, "Stone Butch", *could possibly pass for a man. Spits out words like hand grenades; nearly at the breaking point.*

CLIFF, *drifter type, drunk on hope with a half pound of amazing weed in his backpack. Would probably be considered bi-sexual.*

ROBERTA, *strong black woman with the tirades to prove it. The most well dressed and educated Freedom Fighting Hustler you can think of.*

TANO, *half of the "Snap Queen Team", Puerto Rican, fiercely territorial, able to cut a bitch in half with a single wit.*

MIKA, *other half of the "Snap Queen Team". Not as fast as* TANO, *but probably smarter. Black, tells it like it is, calls it like he sees it; sees the glitz and glamour through tinted shades.*

COP, *Good Ol'Boy just trying to do right by the law. Has never questioned the "Right" or "Wrong" behind what he's ordered to do. Amazing at the intimidation factor of his job.*

MADELINE, *PEG's sister. Has no business being at the riot. Must host a brunch in the morning and has no time for civil rights or emotional outbursts. Secret smoker, terrible driver, has-had-enough.*

THE BAND, *underscores much of the show. Should be guitar, drums and base. A racially diverse proto-punk, dirty, loose and loud trio.*

"/" in between dialogue means the next character has already spoken, creating **overlaps.**

There are a LOT of these in the play.

(I Was There)

(Direct address:)

CARSON: "I was there".
Everybody says that.
After reality, after fact, after that—
people just line up,
"I did it, that was me, I was there".
…If every sissy who said she was at Stonewall
was actually at Stonewall
shit, you coulda seen that rainbow from outer space,
please.
Bitches I've never even heard of just come crawling out
the cracks,
trying to tell me facts and information,
like they were there,
homely looking homosexuals,
please.
…Now some people said some whiteboy threw a
trashcan through the window—
that started it.
Or a stone-butch fought cops off her back, some twinks
lit a Molotov cocktail, everybody started screaming, all
at the same time, the same second, Jesus Christ *It's like
Woodstock.*
And I should know.
Cause I was there too.

TANO: Bullshit.

COP: The reports of what happened next are not exactly
clear.

ROBERTA: You know about Stonewall, /right? Yeah yeah uh-huh, I was *there.*

TANO: You'd have to see it to / believe it, enorme pape, enorme, *of course* I was there

CLIFF: I was there, / right in the thick of it, Friday night, right up to *here.*

MIKA: Saturday Morning *you know* I was there getting all up in it I don't *give a damn* who knows it

MADELINE: It was all just one big fat four day fuckfest

COP: I was there.

CLIFF: I was there.

NEWBIE: I was there too.

PEG: People got lots of different stories.
Everybody was there. Everybody saw something. So what.

MADELINE: So what

COP: So what we have now are the facts, and the facts are the facts but after that

NEWBIE: After that—

TANO: After that—

MIKA: After that—

A-GAY: Honestly; I was blitzed.

NEWBIE: There's a lot of he said, she said, "we all said", but when that's all over

COP: The reports of what happened next are not exactly clear.

CARSON: That first night is the only thing I can still remember shot-by-shot-by second by second.

PEG: Drilled straight into my skull, un-retractable

CARSON & PEG: I was there.

MADELINE: ....1969, New York City.

PEG: The Village.

CARSON: /Greenwich

PEG: /New York City

MIKA: Christopher /street ran straight down that way

A-GAY: Right across the /street from my apartment *very* posh, *very* modern, *very* now.

CLIFF: There was a lamp post / where the light never came on

MADELINE: Oh, and you could see Sheridan Park if you stood/ at the corner

EVERYONE: Sheridan SQUARE

MADELINE: /"Sheridan Square", right over there

CLIFF: Christopher Park /was the big one, Washington and 7th intersected around that way

COP: Difficult to navigate, impossible to get around

ROBERTA & PEG: A bitch to get wherever you're going

MADELINE: 53 Christopher Street

COP: 10014

CLIFF: New / York City

ROBERTA: Greenwich / Village

A-GAY: Middle of / the street

MADELINE: Across from / the park

TANO: Sign sticking / straight up

MIKA: Big letters

NEWBIE: You could / see it down the block

PEG: Huge sign, / couldn't miss it

MIKA: Anybody who's anybody met everybody right outside

CARSON: Stonewall.

(The sign lights up.)

(Everybody snaps to life.)

ROBERTA: Across the street from the Stonewall Inn

CARSON: Christopher Park.

NEWBIE: Friday, June 27th.

CLIFF: Noon

MIKA: 92 Degrees

TANO: Speedo-shorts and bare knees

MIKA: 1969,

TANO & MIKA: Bitch.

(Hot Fun In The Summertime)

(Everyone dissolves, making the space. MIKA and TANO drink.)

(Music. We're there.)

(MIKA and TANO lean on a park fencepost, surveying their territory.)

(They watch the passersby. They've been doing this for years.)

MIKA & TANO: ………………

(NEWBIE crosses.)

TANO: Funny. Or serious?

MIKA: Funny.

TANO: Serious.

MIKA: Way he walks way / he moves

TANO: Glides, *even*

MIKA: *Flies* down the street just two feet shit more like he's got wings, *even*

TANO: Fairy wings, *even*

MIKA: Broke-down-harpy

TANO: Broke down que?

MIKA: Harpy he's a harpy

TANO: Que es un harpy?

MIKA: Some bitch with a twitching ass flying by *my* street on fairy wings, read the goddamn newspaper / bean-queen

TANO: Ohhhhhh, 'ta muy caliente para esa mierda cabrona.

MIKA: Bring down the hands, / bring down the snaps—

TANO: It's too hot for this shit you gotta keep it cool, bitch.

MIKA: If you can't take the heat then don't make me turn the flame on!

NEWBIE: Hey.

MIKA & TANO: …………

NEWBIE: Can I? Can I just? Is there room?

MIKA & TANO: …………………

TANO: "Is there room"

MIKA: Where—

TANO: Right here?

MIKA: With us?

TANO: Is there room / right here with us?

MIKA: HELLLLLLLL no

EVERYONE: ……………

NEWBIE: But… But I just—

TANO: Ay, coño, destruye esa pendeja.

MIKA: Listen you little Newbie, Golden Boy, Howdy-doody / button-down fatherfucker

TANO: Goldie-Hawn / looking wonder-slut

MIKA: This is *our* stoop, this is *our* spot, you don't like the pot then spit out the smoke and cough

TANO: Or better yet get off our turf and go down / to the next block

MIKA: *Mmmmmmmhmm*, So-ho with the homo's talking and the lesbo's eatin' ho-ho's going po-mo

TANO: That means *post-modern* luke-warm nasty pendeja.

MIKA: We need your cracker ass here like we need a hole in our heads

TANO: So get your chitty-chitty-bang-bang-booty back to Westchester County

MIKA: And never approach us with your nonsense ever ever ever again

TANO: I am Tano Rodrigez Santana "Hope" De La Cruz

MIKA: And people just call me Mika

TANO: This is our stoop

MIKA: Dig it or dig out

TANO: Pop, crackle, SNAP, bitch!

(MIKA *and* TANO *drink.*)

NEWBIE: —I was just gonna say—that I liked your outfits. *(He crosses to* BAND.*)*

MIKA: —Actually, that's kind of cute

TANO: Oh I know papi, he's gonna be my husband number one.

MIKA: Stop counting!

TANO: Keep up!

(ROBERTA *appears, out of nowhere, arms full of pamphlets.*)

ROBERTA: Hello hello hello my Brothers,
I'd like you to take a second for W-I-L-D, we're the
groovy /new way to

TANO: Get /the hell away from me

MIKA: Do not pass go do not /collect *anything* for me,
EVEN.

TANO: Don't let the puerta hit you where the perra bit
you.

ROBERTA: (*Crossing to the phone*)
......This is a public park, y'all don't own shit,
so while you two keep bitchin,
I'm gonna start stichin the fabric of the future,
ten cents my brothers, ten cents is all it takes—
Y'all go 'bout your day now,
(*On the phone*)
Hello hello, this is Roberta baby, /
just reminding you about the W-I-L-D meeting this
afternoon, that's right, W-I-L-D at three-thirty right
here in Christopher Park, dig on that, ha-ha!
(*Hangs up phone and exits.*)

TANO: Ay, Dios mio, mi Dios madre del verbo.

MIKA: I hate when they just ATTACK you

TANO: She does /not KNOW me

MIKA: Angela Davis got her afro on way too tonight, /
Shit, coming up on me

TANO: WALK, bitch, WALK, /bitch, WALK, bitch

MIKA: Get your ass back to Sarah Lawrence girl,
MOVE!

TANO: Oh-oh-OH! Incoming, twelve o'clock, INCOMING.
—Funny / or serious?

(CLIFF *passes by.*)

MIKA: Hysterical Homosexuality baby, / *Laugh-In*

TANO: *Nonono* Honey he's *dead-serious,* / you don't even know

MIKA: Look at that / backpack, the boots, the hair, *no man* wants *that man*

TANO: No no *see,* You don't even *understand,* see, / ese un *wayward*

MIKA: Yeah-huh, way towards homo-alley

TANO: You're / blind as a bitch.

MIKA: Tano I can see I can *tell* gimme one look baby / one look that's all it takes

TANO: No, no, no, *see,* he's got *history,* Okay, probably a construction worker or a factory builder or an angel or a math teacher or somebody who uses their hands a lot, / HISTORY.

MIKA: Hand-job-jiver

TANO: He's Wow Now, / *Oh* so wow-now

MIKA: Man I'm / wow-now

TANO: Siempre 'ta pegao como una pulga en culo el perro

MIKA: I'm *wow now,* gimme some.

TANO: Mika baby I wouldn't give you some of anything if you were the last man on earth.

MIKA: Yeah well I am the last man on earth everyone else with a cock is just a dick.

TANO: And no matter how much a rooster peacock's he's still just another shrill-screaming cock on the block hawking rocks dropping shop mocking shock wearing some mock ugly-frock begging for slop.

MIKA & TANO: ....

MIKA: ...I *like it!*

TANO: You /like that one?!

MIKA: I *like it,* so-fast-girl!

TANO: So fast!

MIKA & TANO: Stairway-to-straight-shot-baby!
Jinx,
Shit,
Drink!
(They've already pulled out hidden flasks, they drink!)

TANO: Hold it / hold it now, incoming

MIKA: Oh *honey*

TANO: You see that?

MIKA: This Queen thinks shes Cleopatra but she's really just Liz Taylor.

TANO: Bug off, Bitch!

(CARSON passes, in full black funeral regalia.)

(MIKA and TANO don't move a muscle...)

TANO: Funny /or *seriously* funny

MIKA: *Seriously father-fucking-funny!*

TANO: *(Cracking up)* Ay, Coño, me muero de la risa. Casi me meo encima.

MIKA: Honey I had no idea his kind could walk around in the sunlight, vampiric lookin *sea-bitch*

TANO: Sea-bitch!

MIKA: Riddle me this, when's the last time you think he got dick

TANO: Time?

MIKA: And place

TANO: That alley, three minutes ago

MIKA: Ass ain't even dry yet, /shit, bet his ass is never dry

TANO: Bet his ass is never dry, /BEAT you, BEAT you!

MIKA: Oh *you're getting quick* bitch!

TANO: YOU GET ME

(MIKA *and* TANO *do a secret-handshake.*)

MIKA: Straight /*sideways* I get you

TANO: That's right baby

MIKA & TANO:
Shiiiiiiiiiiiiiiit.
Jinx!
Drink!

CARSON: Look upon me.
Behold
a true-blue bitch
through and through.
…Look upon one who has seen the end and cross
yourselves in fear of the eternal damnation and
repercussanial happenstance that awaits the fate of the
fakes who try to put me in my place,
Lookuponmemotherfucker
I. Know. You. *Well.*
You, black-thing, mandingo, tank-top, speedo,
You, Guido, Latino, *el stupido*
bottom, bottom feeder,
Never met a dick you couldn't lick,
Never met a dick you didn't like,
I know your type,
Creeping like a cockroach in the night out of mind out
of sight cause y'all sisses *just don't look right* in the light,
Hell I've seen better bitches uptown at the dogpound

before the city puts em down,
You mouth-breathing pimple-popping pot-pushing no-
dicked hypocrites,
get off my stoop get out my park and go roll around in
the dark
go
and troll
and bark with the rest of the mutts who slut it up
after dusk ya pencil-dicked-half-slit-pocket-broke-
beer-bellied-cock-eyed-limp-wristed-ass-swishin-day-
drinkin-un-thinking-lilly-livered-fish-smelling-*faggots.*

EVERYONE: ………….

TANO: Look, Mister

CARSON: I am *not* a mister.

MIKA: Oh, *shit.*

TANO: *(To* MIKA*)* —I've *got* this. *(To* CARSON*)* Okay, hi,
I'm Tano Rodrigez Santana "Hope" de la Cruz of one-
hundred-and-ten-street, six foot, switch-hitter, Gemini,
hi—
…Whatever *you* are?
You got guts.
Walking around in the daylight, looking like t*hat,*
lookiing like—
(—my God, girl, go with it—)
—So you're quick. Quicker than me. Congratulations.
But that's it. That's *it.*
Mika and me? When we go out? We're looking to *ball,*
we don't buy drinks. I get them, and he gets them,
but you don't; So you have to be Bitchy.
Cause that's all you have.
That's why you gotta dress like that,
look like that, como la puerca de Juan Bobo
next time you tuck your dick in between your legs *leave
some room to walk,*
bow-legged *bitch,*

tricky black witch,
grab a spike dust if off and sit
—And while you're at it!
——fuck off!
Cause if you expect us to carry you around like a float
then you're gonna wind up carried out DEAD, like that
drunk tub of guts Judy Garland, if *you ever*

(CARSON *slaps* TANO.)

(*Once, twice, three times*))

EVERYONE: …………..

CARSON: Apologize.

TANO: What—

CARSON: Apologize

TANO: I'm sorry, sorrysorry, I'm sorry!

CARSON: …….That's correct.

(CARSON *quickly disappears.*

TANO *stands, stunned.*)

MIKA: ………*hahahah*HAHAHAHAH /
HAHAHAHAHAHAHAHAH

TANO: Oh that's right, uh huh, / get your yucks in,
come on bitch.

MIKA: She snapped your ass in HALF.

TANO: I cut her good

MIKA: You didn't cut shit bitch—

This is Judy Garland day, like it or not. My boss heard
she up and died? Went *nutso;* made me put on A Star Is
Born,
cried all day,
tequila, tequila, tequila.

TANO: Judy Fucking Garland is Fatherfucking dead,
Mika. DEAD.

…Never saw *Wizard of Oz*, never saw *A Star is Born*, I
only listen to *far-out-real shit,*
The Beatles, The Stooges, The Bee Gees, These bitches /
(whoever they even are)

THE BAND: Yeah! / Far out! /Woooo!

TANO: Judy Garland, que ha hecho esa puta por mi?
NADA!
She's DEAD.

MIKA: Yeah, and that shits *kind of a big deal*

TANO: For WHO.
She wasn't
one of us.

MIKA: …Who the hell is us?

MIKA & TANO: ………

ROBERTA: *(Direct address:)*
Hello hello hello my brothers and sisters,
y'all got a second for W-I-L-D, the ice-cold-red-hot-
new-shit you gotta get with,
just one second in one second Roberta's gonna turn
your whole world around,
hot day outside today, HOT day,
step right up and cool off in the knowledge of the ever-
expanding-mind-blowing-heart-stopping *wow,*
now, YES it is hot as hell outside,
YES we got a lunatic in the White House using your
money to wipe his ass,
YES our mothers are mourning our brothers down in
Vietnam dropping bomb after bomb after bomb,
YES Judy Garland is DEAD, but we are ALIVE my
brothers and sisters, let us not mourn, let us be reborn,
can I get a witness (amen) sock it to me now all right
I'm here all week, people! I'm big, I'm black, and you
can bet your ass I'm hard to ignore, W.I.L.D on the

loose, *truth* on the loose, hold me back now, Roberta, OUT!

(Direct address)

(CARSON crosses through the scene.)

TANO: Across town.

MIKA: 81st Street between Madison and Fifth Avenue

NEWBIE: Frank E Campbell Funeral Chapel

MIKA: The Waiting Room

TANO: No air conditioning

CLIFF: 1:30 P M.

CARSON: Judy Garland's Dead Body.

(Funeral Chapel)

(We're in the waiting room. A few chairs. CARSON sits.)

(CLIFF enters with a large duffel bag. He takes a minute—he feels out the room. He's anything but low.)

CLIFF: …Immense bummer, right?

CARSON: …………..

CLIFF: Lots of people, yeah? Lots and lots and—
Say about two thousand? Three thousand?
Three, yeah?

CARSON: ………………

CLIFF: Is that one of her's?
The dress?

CARSON: *(Almost a smile)* ……………..

CLIFF: Ha! Thought so.
Looks outta this world, lady, real far out.
Spitting image.

CARSON: …We share the same birthday.

CLIFF: Wow.

CARSON: Well, she was older, surely.
I mean, *surely.*

CLIFF: …You heard how, right?
Some heavy, heavy, heavy hardcore drugs.

CARSON: —Where'd you hear that?

CLIFF: New York Times?

CARSON: Shitrag. It wasn't drugs, NO.
It was accidental.
—Over a long period of time.
It was a long, long accident.

CLIFF: You happy with this?

CARSON: —It feels right.
There's nothing—*right* about this, but—it feels —
classy.
…What's your favorite film?

CLIFF: Uh. *Wizard of Oz?*

CARSON: ……………

CLIFF: I don't see a lot of movies.
I'm a—I'm / a busy guy, you know?

CARSON: Mmmmhmmm,
You're *without,* aren't you?

CLIFF: What? "Without" what?

CARSON: That's not my blank to fill in.

CLIFF: I'm a *traveler.*

CARSON: Mmmmhmm.

CLIFF: India, Amsterdam, Paris, /the hills of Northern
China

CARSON: And that actually means—

CLIFF: Ohio, Iowa, *Jersey.*

CARSON: *Jersey. Oh.* Parasitical life-form.

CLIFF: Sucked-my-LIFE out,
cops tried to bust me in Newark? Just looking like this,
like-this,
WHAT, I think I look pretty damn solid.

CARSON: They'd love me

CLIFF: Fuck the pigs. I'm way too fast to fall behind
their bullshit, know what I mean?

CARSON: Oh please.

CLIFF: Pigs can't catch shit, see, I've got *moves*.

CARSON: Now they don't play.
If they catch you—they got you.

CLIFF: And I'm telling you, I'm FAST, /see, they

CARSON: When they got you it doesn't matter how fast
you were.
Who you *were*.
They find you, lock you in, take you uptown,
and everything you *were* or were *trying to* be or
whatever secrets you *have*,
it's *out*,
they take your picture, put it in the paper, and
everybody knows what you *are*.
You think you're fast? When they come, you better run
faster. You better break the god-damn speed-limit.

CLIFF: …You're tough as shit.

CARSON: Oh, / *don't*.

CLIFF: I'm serious! You're pretty fucking far out.

CARSON: I never go by far out, only incredible—

CLIFF: Fucking Incredible.

CARSON & CLIFF: ………………………

CARSON: (*A quick break*) …Don't look at me *stop stop*
don't
look at me, / like that.

CLIFF: —Like /what

CARSON: *(Trying not to laugh)* Like that! Stop!

CLIFF: My fault.
….Are you always —*up* like that?

CARSON: —Weekends and special occasions.

CLIFF: So during any other day—

CARSON: You wouldn't recognize what's underneath
this if you bumped into me on an empty street.

CLIFF: Doubt that.

CARSON: *I* don't recognize me.

CLIFF: …Want me to walk you home after this?
Just—you know—just in case?
I have another uh—coat. In my backpack. / Shoes, too,
so if—

CARSON: *I am not* going to see my idol dressed in
slacks, a tie,
I am going to see her *as I am*
Because how on earth is she supposed to recognize me,
if I'm hiding?
—She made me feel. So. Much. Less—ugly……
I am *not* taking off this dress.
Not until tonight is over, and she is down in the
ground, and she is at peace,
it's *proper*.
—I'm not slipping this off my shoulders, so help me
God above.

CLIFF: You really loved her, didn't you?

CARSON & CLIFF: ………

CARSON: *(A slow crack)* She.
She. She didn't get—
—I'm sorrry, /sorry, I'm sorry—

CLIFF: Shh, *no, no*, get it out, let it fall, let it fall.

CARSON: She didn't get to see *the rest* of it.
And I worry. I worry *so, so much.*

CLIFF: What do you worry about?

CARSON: *(Overcome with emotion)* ...I worry about Liza

CLIFF: No, /no no no, don't worry about Liza, she's
gonna be fine

CARSON: She always look so confused and troubled
and /*erratic and lost*

CLIFF: She's tough, she's gonna /be fine

CARSON: She'll be dead by the time she's thirty goddamn-it

CLIFF: She's got her Dad, her Dad's great—

CARSON: Her Dad's a faggot

CLIFF: SO ARE YOU!

CARSON & CLIFF: !!!!!!!!

CLIFF: ......You never told me your name.

CARSON: ...Carson.

CLIFF: —*Carson?* Like—like Johnny, *no, no,* what the
hell kind of name is that for a

CARSON: A what?

CLIFF: —Strong confident woman such as yourself?

CARSON: Carson by day, whatever you want by night,
now who the hell are you?

CLIFF: Cliff.

CARSON: Mmmhmm. "And what the hell kind of name
is that for / a"

CLIFF: A draft dodging young son of a gun like the guy
in front of you?

CARSON: ...God above

CLIFF: No biggie. They drafted me. Didn't go. So.

CARSON: What

CLIFF: Come on, you want me to scream it?
This April. Shit happens.

CARSON: And when shit happens, you tell the
recruiting people you're a dick-sucking-swish,
you get off the hook

CLIFF: Then everybody knows

CARSON: If the shoe fits

CLIFF: It doesn't, *I'm not*, I…
I don't *know*……
Look.
(He takes CARSON's *hand.)*
I didn't just come here for—her, okay.
Saw you today. That park in Greenwich?
Saw you telling off those creepy little bitches, *I saw*
that—
and I just————I had to know what could happen.
Had to know who the hell that was.
For the first time,
in my life, I thought—

*(*MADELINE *appears.)*

MADELINE: *(Beyond abrupt)* We took a poll.
….Excuse me?
Well. Well, this is, um, this / is very

CLIFF: You need something?

MADELINE: We took *a poll*—
my—my friends and I, we're— (we're right over there,
next to the window,)
and we've been here for hours and hours and hours
and
it's hot and it's sticky just muggy and I never do this I
never say this I never—
I need to tell you to
please

refrain from—
I need to tell you to keep your hands to yourself,
I need to tell you to stop with the touching,
I need to tell you to stop doing what you're doing
or I'm going to have to call someone to deal with it
now I'm sorry to be the bearer of the bad news but
it's hot and it's a sad day and you're making people
uncomfortable and we took a poll.

CARSON: Excuse me. But if what we're doing over here
is making you /uncomfortable

MADELINE: Please.
Don't—don't look at me when you speak.

CLIFF: Hey, look here lady *you know what*—

CARSON: *(Without camp. Complete, programed respect)*
I'm very sorry ma'am. Please accept my apology.
…I'm sorry for dressing like this. Sorry for letting this
man touch me.
Won't happen again, Ma'am.

MADELINE: …….That's correct. (She turns back around.

CARSON starts pulling her things together.)

CARSON: *I told you,* you're never/*to ever*

CLIFF: *I'm not supposed to be* **breathing.** Okay?

You're right. And, and if the pigs catch you, right here,
right now,
you're going to jail. And that's horrible.
—If I get caught? I get on a plane. And they send me
over there.
And I go, into the jungle, and the patties, and the black
and I die.
And I will die. Guys in my family? We don't *win* war,
we *die, but* I. Don't. *Care.*
Because if if they bust in and take us right now? Least I
did what I wanted to do,
least I did it my way before they took me away.

Now allright, I have no clue what it's like to be you—
but long as I'm around?
Fuck what the pigs say, fuck what that Jackie-O-
lameass says, fuck all of that noise—
We're gonna do whatever the hell we want.
Know why?
....Cause I'm gonna meet Judy Garland.

CARSON: Please—

CLIFF: I was sniffing around?
And right to the left of that door there's a hallway. And
round the corner from that there's another door.
Behind that other door?
—I heard music.

CARSON: *(Overwhelmed)* ......God above.
Oh my God above.

CLIFF: If you let me take you back there......will you let
me take you to a bar?
And let you let me buy you a drink?

CARSON: ......

CLIFF: Sorry, will you let me get *someone else* to buy me
a drink which I will then give to you cause goddamn-it
lady you're worth it.

CARSON: ...Rum and coke. Hold the ice. And the coke.

CLIFF: Let me take your hand.

CARSON: ...I **told you,** people-don't

CLIFF: Just until it stops shaking.

*(...*CLIFF *takes* CARSON's *hand.)*

(They exit side by side.)

*(*COP *enters. He watches* CLIFF *and* CARSON *exit, hand in
hand.)*

(Direct address.)

COP: 3:30 that afternoon.
Back in the village?
96 degrees.

MIKA: No air conditioning

TANO: Shirts are *this* close to coming off

MIKA & TANO:
Christopher Park
Shit,
Jinx,
DRINK!

(Christopher Park)

(MIKA and TANO drink.)

COP *hangs around, lights a cigarette.)*

TANO: Ten o'clock

MIKA: What /ten o'clock where's ten o'clock *that ain't*
ten o'clock we're on Easten Standard Time *up here*

TANO: Right there, THAT, Coño e como tener un hijo
retardo *(morón)* allí THAT.

MIKA: Oh-My-God

TANO: Incoming.

(They freeze. PEG approaches.)

PEG: —Hey.

MIKA & TANO: ......

PEG: I—I'm—I don't know how to do this, uh—
I lost my wallet.
And. I don't know I dunno what to do right now you
got like a dime or something gotta gotta make a call or
something,
you know?

MIKA & TANO: ......

PEG: Guys deaf or something?
......See you two here all day all the time you see me
come on comeonwhatthefuck,
you guys hear me?

TANO: Don't say anything. —It'll go away.

PEG: ...Know what? Everyday, I walk by here, and you
two, just, talk *so much shit*, bout me, bout everybody,
and YOU KNOW WHAT—

COP: Hey.

PEG: —Hey.

COP: Hot out here, yeah?

(MIKA *and* TANO *take a step back.*)

(*They watch.*)

PEG: Yeah, yeahman, I—horrible, horrible /god-damn-
day-today

COP: Muggy as hell, right?
You Need some help with something?

PEG: Yeah, so, uh—so I'm getting off the train, right,
and I grab for my wallet and I grabbed for it and it
wasn't there /so now I'm—

COP: Hey—slow down, slow down, it's all right—
slow down.
Start at the top.

PEG & COP: ....

PEG: —Got off the train.
Felt something.
Grabbed.
Wallet. Somebody took it.
Gotta get home.
....Just need a dime man. And I know it's—it's fucking
hot and everybody's got something else to do,
but it's just one of those days, you know, but I really—

COP: Fuck are you?

PEG: —Scuse /me

COP: Don't interrupt me, said what the fuck are you?

PEG: …

COP: I stutter?
You hear me—

PEG: *(Almost an exit)* DONE

COP: **HEY.**
……..You shouldn't come around here anymore.

PEG: Why the hell not?

COP: I said so—

PEG: And I said *why the hell not* what are you like a—

COP: Concerned citizen.

PEG: —Oh yeah?

COP: Yeah. That's it.

PEG: Great, cause I'm not a bum, I'm not some dumb
kid I'm just somebody asking a concerned civilian for
some help.
You got a dime or am I wasting my time?

COP: …Come over here.

(PEG approaches. Stops a few feet away.)

PEG: ………

COP: Come on get over here, get over here.

PEG: …Look

COP: *(Suddenly grabs her, pulling her close)* No, / listen—

PEG: Get /OFFAme

COP: *Listen,* I know what you are, what you really
are. And I'm not the smartest guy in the world, so, if I
know—everybody else knows too.
You're not fooling anybody, so I'd advise you HEY—

I'd advise you to put on something a little more made
up,
or else settle with the fact that somebody
a lot less nice then me—
might do something not too nice to somebody dressed
just like that.
Heat like this? Makes people crazy.
am I making myself clear?
AM I MAKING. MYSELF. / CLEAR—

PEG: *(Calling over to* MIKA *and* TANO*)* Hey, HEY—

TANO: HEY......
Step off, all right?

COP: What?

TANO: ....

MIKA: Nothing.

COP: ....You see?
They don't do anything, they watch, now *do you hear
me? Trying to help you out kid, all-right?
All-right?*

PEG: All-right.

COP: *Good*...... Go home. Change your clothes. Don't
walk around this park my kids play in dressed like
that,
round here, ever again, you got that?

PEG: —I—

COP: "I got that."

PEG: ..."I got that."

COP: Good. Call your mother or something.
*(Throws a quarter on the ground.
Lights a cigarette. Exits)*

*(*PEG *stares at the quarter.
She doesn't pick it up. She's motionless, still.)*

MIKA: God damn fatherfucking freak

TANO: Did you see the way / he looked at me

MIKA: He's always outside the bar, never inside, never ever inside—
Last week? Saw him walking around, right outside Manhole. Sniffin.
Tuesday night? Pigs raided Manhole.

TANO: Era Martes cabrona.
The only people in Manhole on Tuesday are trolls, and witches, and fairies,
take the whole Enchanted fucking forest, carajo
/ you're trying to tell me

TANO: Tano, listen, TANO, I'm trying to tell you that *he's the one.*
The one that makes it happen?
….He walks in some bar, checks it out, next day the whole place gets paddywaggoned.
Guys like that are gonna be the end of us, I'm telling you,
you see them up here,
you *keep-low.*
You *watch.*

(They stare at PEG.)

TANO: *(Bendita)* Poor dumb dyke.

MIKA: Don't get involved don't say "stop" just go about your business.
Just the way and the will of the world we're living in.

TANO: …Oh, Mika……Malcom X is not a good look for you *chica.*

MIKA: Oh Go-to-hell-Fatherfucker

TANO: *(Flicking him off)* Oh I brought back a brochure / for ya yeah, did you get it?

MIKA: *(Flicking him off)* Yeah-uh-huh I got my copy in my mailbox waiting

(ROBERTA *enters.*)

ROBERTA: Hello Hello my sister,
you must be here for the three-thirty meeting of W-I-L-D,
well you came to the right place sister girl just
simmer down for one second that's all it takes in just
one second we can get you on the right track to the
righteous and the uplifted—

PEG: —Sorry—

ROBERTA: Take a pamphlet.

PEG: —I'm. / I'm not—

ROBERTA: Oh don't worry this isn't your every-other-day-women's-rights-holiday this is TODAY, baby,
tomorrow is just constantly happening!
…Are you okay?

PEG: …….

ROBERTA: Oh! You drop a quarter?
Here—

PEG: No

ROBERTA: Oh just / take it

PEG: I CAN'T.

PEG & ROBERTA: …………

ROBERTA: —Well you know what you can do?
Listen-to-*me*!
I'm a great talker I tell it like it is how it goes what it
do when it do and I do it damn well, I'm Roberta baby
and *I know* what's cracking,
pop a squat, let's put the power to the hour,
Welcome to your first meeting of W-I-L-D baby!

(MIKA *and* TANO *quickly exit.*)

TANO: Carajo, llama la policia que se lleven las putas esas pa'allá!

MIKA: Not again, I can't stand her, / every day "she's out and she's loud and she's out and loud about it", PLEASE.

ROBERTA: Yeah, that's right, get-to-stepping I'm starting a revolution while y'all just prostituting, uh-huh that's right, WALK!

(MIKA *and* TANO *are gone.*)

ROBERTA: So! Hey! This is Wild,
and Wild stands for Women Internationally Learning Divisiveness.
You dig,all-right, check it: We're all about women internationally learning divisiveness.
Right? *Right on*, sister.
Now this isn't one of those "sit around in a circle holding hands crying about our Mommies" things you see over at N Y U,
nuh-uh
we're not about the love in,
we're about the *love-ing*
with-in,
(you feel me?)
we're about looking *inside* of *ourselves,*
getting to know *that,*
respecting that,
love-ing with-in that,
and *then*
looking outside of ourselves and going "Say WHAT now? HELL no. Things gotta change, I mean DAMN!"
You *feel* me? *You* feel me.

PEG: —Is this about lesbians?

ROBERTA: Baby, this is about Women Internationally Learning Divisiveness.
…(And if you take that to mean two sisters getting to

know each other in the process, go ahead and go with
it.) Okay! Now I'm gonna talk about the man.
First rule of WILD: "Fight the man".
And not the man as in the man with the plan, the man
ever-present and always above,
the man who is *with-in*, *love-ing*, Jesus Christ,
hell no, not *that* man,
the man I'm talking about is the man with the book,
not the good book, the book that gets thrown,
I'm talking about the man with the bat, the pigs, cause
you know what the
Second rule of WILD is?
We ain't afraid of no cops, we don't believe their lies,
we slash their tires when they start acting up,
making em slow down, making em think twice,
now can you shovel what I'm digging sister?
This is about looking BEYOND ourselves,
with-in, love-ing,
see now *I knew* you felt me,
Okay, the final rule of WILD?
You ready for this?
Final Rule of Wild—Do not trust the gays.
look over there.

(We see NEWBIE *enter, alone.)*

(He lights up a joint.)

ROBERTA: They *rile shit up.*
They're loud, they're crazy, and *I know* you know the
reason we got so many police shuffling around parks
is cause they can't keep their peens in their pants. *(Also
they don't share their green which makes me PISSED; damn
selfish-ass fairy-fuckers,)*
So
I'm here here to tell you that if Woman are to learn
how to achieve Divisiveness Internationally,
we gotta say "hold it boys, we're driving this next
revolution,

you can sit shotgun if you're so excited, but ***don't you
dare*** tell us directions because we know exactly where
we going so put the map down and maybe turn the
music up so we can get our groove on, okay?"
Damn the man. Fuck the pigs. Hold off the boys.
Those are the rules.
What'd you think?

PEG: —I still think this is about lesbians.

ROBERTA: Okay look,
I don't call myself a lesbian,
I call myself a dyke
don't call me a lesbian, my Grandma was a lesbian

PEG: Really?

ROBERTA: No, but you know what I mean!
That word's over, done, dead, bury it in the back.
We gotta start standing up for ourselves, taking the
words they throw at us,
and owning them.
I'm a dyke.
I'm a nigger.
I'm a woman, what else you got, bring it on, say it to
me.
......I'm not allowed to go to Women's Movement
meeting's anymore 'cause I told them that their march
speeches should include women of color.
They said "No. The movement is too fragile."
So I said "You tell me when the movement is
stronger, cause I'm gonna join an organization that's
about EQUAL rights, COMPASSIONATE politics,
UNIVERSAILITY."
......So I went to the Black Panthers.
And the Black Panthers hated me more then the
Women's Movement!
They can't screw me, so they don't wanna see me,
they—

………..
…Look I know this is crazy, you're sitting here, with a
one-woman-coalition,
somebody who nobody wants,
I know, it's bonkers,
but….but this is all I have.
This is about being the best,
proudest, strongest women you can be,
the woman you know you can be,
the woman you deserve to be.

PEG: …You ever—
You ever feel

ROBERTA: So god damn alone that you shut right down
and try to shut everybody else out too?
I don't.

PEG: Really.

ROBERTA: Mmmmhmmm

PEG: Well where do you go when you—
when you can't go anywhere anymore,
when you can't go to your fucking "movement
meetings" and you don't have any family anymore and
you're just you, what then, what happens?

ROBERTA: You start your own shit.
That's what happens.
So. We've gotta help each other, right?

PEG: Right.

ROBERTA: Now spit it to me sister.

PEG: Rule Number One, down with the man, /uh. no,
sorry, right, right right, uh—

ROBERTA: No no that's Black Panthers, they can go to
hell, DAMN the man, /that's what we do

PEG: DAMN the man, rule number one

ROBERTA: Rule number two, /Fuck the pigs

PEG: FUCK the pigs

ROBERTA: Fuck 'em, and rule number three—

PEG: Don't trust the gays

ROBERTA: That's W-I-L-D baby! See! Tomorrow is just constantly happening!

PEG: What does your movement say about kissing?

ROBERTA: What does what now—

(PEG *kisses* ROBERTA.)

PEG & ROBERTA: …………………..

PEG: I wanted to do that since the second I saw you, but you never fucking shut up.

ROBERTA: *(Totally surprised)* …Well I ain't got shit to say now.

PEG: Stonewall.

ROBERTA: What /about it

PEG: Stonewall. Eleven-thirty. Dance room, tonight, all right?

ROBERTA: —Stonewall?!

PEG: YES, right across / the fucking street

ROBERTA: But that's a man bar! I mean a gay bar! *(I mean damn I gotta watch myself)*

PEG: See ya there

ROBERTA: Should I call you?

PEG: Call me Peg! *(Exits)*

(MIKA *and* TANO *re-enter with bags.)*

ROBERTA: *(Waving, yelling off)*
Right, Peg! Right!
—Hey!
HEY!
PEG! I'M CALLING YOU PEG!

I GET IT!
HAHAHAAHA!
HEY PEG!
"Grazing in the grass is a gas, baby can you dig it," OH!
*"I can dig it, he can dig it, she can dig it, we can dig it, they
can dig it, you can dig it, baby, can you—"*

MIKA, ROBERTA & TANO: ………………..

MIKA & TANO: ….*Mmmmhmmmm.*

ROBERTA: *(Telling it like it is)* …Judge me all you want:
Y'all just sick cause I'm the only heffa up here who's
actually gonna *get fucked t*onight. / HA! Dig on that,
bitches!

MIKA & TANO: OH SHIT, OH SHIT NO-SHE-DIDN'T
/ En el nombre del padre, del hijo, y del espiritu santo.
Rezo por la vida de esas lesbianas pecadoras.

ROBERTA: MMMMMMhmmmmmmmmm! *(She exits,
yelling off.)* Who wants to get W-I-L-D that's right ladies
W-I-L-D all-day all the way strong baby! *(She's gone.)*

TANO: —What is WRONG with your people?!

MIKA: I'd ask you the same question but I already saw
West Side Story.

TANO: Well, she ain't with me

MIKA: Nobody's "with you", Tano.
Nobody's with any of us.
We're just here, we're just bitching, we're just single,
dig it or dig out.

TANO: …We gotta ball.

MIKA: It is hot-as-hell, /I'm tired, I'm woozy, can
barely stand up I'm staying IN.

TANO: Cause you woke up and drank the same beer
you fell asleep with,
we-gotta-BALL tonight Mika cause tonight— Tonight?
it's gonna *happen.*

NEWBIE: Yea! It's gonna HAPPEN! / Yea!

TANO: / Oh (shut yourself up before I go over there and do it for you, bitch)

MIKA: *Hell no* keep to yourself mind your own business bitch *mind it!*

TANO: It's all going to happen Mika, TONIGHT! Eleven-fifteen. Incoming. Watch this.

(A-GAY *passes.*)

MIKA: ...Not funny. Not serious.

TANO: Doesn't even register on the Radar.

MIKA & TANO: An A-Gay. (*They drink.*)

(A-GAY *stops in front of* NEWBIE.)

A-GAY: Hey.

NEWBIE: —Hey.

A-GAY: Hey.

NEWBIE: Hey. /I—

A-GAY: Shut up, stand up, stay quiet and follow me.

(A-GAY *exits...*NEWBIE *follows.*)

TANO: *That's* gonna be me.

MIKA: Oh Lord /have mercy, Jesus Christ, *call me back.*

TANO: Fit, aggressive, masculine; one foot in front
of the other my ass staying in one position and not
moving my hands, *at all;*
that's me.
I will be Tano Rodrigez Santana "Hope" Cruz of one-
hundred and twenty first street no longer,
oh no, now, I will be "Terry Robinson Harley of
Waverly Street by the deli",
/ *That's* who I'm gonna be Mika, watch this—

MIKA: White. /White. White, white, white white white
white, white-white-WHITE.

TANO: The bar *will bow to me,* wave to me, come to me,
and I'll dance, with everybody, and I'll fuck, whoever I
want, and—
…And when that freak over there—

MIKA: He's coming back?

TANO: Four-thirty, don't look, he's on your four.
….When he comes up to me and starts poking his
business around when it doesn't belong he's not gonna
look at me.
Cause I look like *that.*

MIKA: But-you-don't

TANO: I could. My elementary school teacher told me
she thought I was Italian.

MIKA: Who was your teacher? Helen Keller?

TANO: It was the lighting, you didn't see the lighting.

MIKA: Spics ain't shit. You know this.

TANO: ….*You* of all /people

MIKA: Know exactly what *those* people think of *my*
people is just a little bit more then they think of *yours.*
Tano? You ain't no A-Gay girl.
To them? The highest we go is a C Plus.
Dig it or dig out.

TANO: …Mika honey? We gotta move on up cause
Jesus Christ *I am sick* of this stoop. Tonight.

MIKA: Gonna be a hundred degrees by then

TANO: Across the street

MIKA: *Jesus* Tano / Jesus

TANO: Stonewall

MIKA: Oh *fuck no,* if I wanted spit in my cocktails I'd do
it myself

TANO: Bring a flask

MIKA: I left my flask at that gay commune on Bleeker street last week / I ain't got no flask now

TANO: Carajo 'ta bien, 'ta bien, 'TA BIEN! I'll bring my flask with me but honey it's all doing down tonight, we're moving on up,
meet back here, midnight: Dress like an A-Gay.

TANO: I'm wearing this.

TANO & MIKA: Out!
(They exit.)

COP: *(Direct Address)* Six-thirty P M.
Day's done.
Ninety-four degrees.
Celsius? Doesn't stop, keeps going up, up up up.
Tourists are just passing through the village now,
back in the hotel by seven seeing a show down the way at eight.
The locals? Nobody's here. Streets are thinning out, people getting ready.
...But They're coming *back.*
Most definitely, swear to God, they will be here tonight.

(Christopher Park)

(COP with a newspaper. CLIFF approaches.)

CLIFF: Got the time man?

COP: —Six-thirty.

CLIFF: *Shit.* On the dot?

COP: On the dot.

CLIFF: *Shit.*
—Supposed to meet up with somebody, ya know—
right here, right now, you know how it is.

COP: ...Some kind of hot date?

CLIFF: Yea—well, *she is*, she's just—
wow, / you know?

COP: *She* is?

CLIFF: She is, yea, *me*? *(I look kinda like something the cat got crazy with)* but she, she's—fucking *rock solid*, man. Ever—you ever meet somebody, and then, just, five minutes later, at that mark, you just look at 'em and you realize "shit—this is it", man, / "this is—"

COP: You get it.

CLIFF: *Exactly* man, *you get me* man—
Uh, met her today, we had a drink, and she said she had to run up to her apartment, to—
That's just the oldest excuse in the book, right, "in a minute," right, I should, just, / I should just beat feet, right, I mean

COP: No, no no that doesn't mean anything, look—
You're a smart kid, right?

CLIFF: Right.

COP: You don't look like it but who cares right?

CLIFF: Right?

COP: Exactly, right, but you're smarter then the rest of these—whatever you call it's, right, you not like them, so don't freak out. K?
—Over there? Sheridan Square?
Met my wife over there, / five years ago

CLIFF: No shit man?

COP: Walking her dog, just out of the blue, boom.
…You never know the second you see someone, it's not like the movies.
You gotta wait a minute.
Piece of advice, one gentleman to another, all right?

CLIFF: Thanks.

COP: Just don't fuck it up.

CLIFF: That from today?
(Nods to the paper)

COP: Absolutely.

CLIFF: Yeah, you read about Cowan in / that yet?

COP: Billy Cowan's an idiot, trade him, / trade him to hell for all I care

CLIFF: Yankee's need somebody though, / give it a few months man, oh, *holy shit*

COP: No, the Yankees are fine, they're always gonna be fine—

CLIFF: *Holy fucking shit*—
HEY. What took you so long?
You look exactly the same.

CARSON: That's what took so long.
Afternoon.

COP: —Evening.
(He starts to exit.)

CARSON: Stonewall tonight?

COP: Stonewall. Tonight.
(He's gone.)

CLIFF: What's Stonewall?

CARSON: The biggest mistake of your life.
Right over there honey.
Only place they let us dance around here. And if I ever / see

CLIFF: —Molly Minelli.

CARSON: What now?

CLIFF: That's your new name, just made it up, you're not Carson anymore, you're Molly Minelli, uh, Liza's long-long-long lost *other* sister

CARSON: Lorna Luft?

CLIFF: Fuck that dishrag, you're *Molly Minelli*, Lorna got the shaft, Liza got the voice, *you* got the looks, that's showbiz kid, right?

CARSON: *(Surrendering a smile)* …I need a drink.

(I Need A Drink)

(We follow various spots in N Y C.)

(They're not literally one group; but the direct address tells us that everyone is in the same tempo, mood and rhythm, if not the same location. The music builds and builds……All direct address.)

PEG & ROBERTA: "Stonewall Inn, /Dance Room, Midnight"

NEWBIE: I need a drink I need a drink /I need a drink

A-GAY, ROBERTA, PEG, CARSON, CLIFF & COP: I need *a drink!*

MIKA & TANO: "Bar Center, / 11 Tonight, better be there, better wear something tight"

NEWBIE & MADELINE: I need a drink I need a drink / I need a drink

EVERYONE: I need *a drink*

CARSON: 53 Christopher Street

NEWBIE: Middle of the block

PEG: Big lights,

ROBERTA: Pointed arrows,

NEWBIE: The biggest thing on the block!

MADELINE: Terrible place.

CARSON: The only place they let us dance.

(Everyone looks towards the STONEWALL sign.)

COP: I need a drink 'cause what I've been planning for two weeks is all going down in two hours.

CARSON: I need a drink because I can't think *right* right now.

MADELINE: I need a drink because as modern as I pretend I am at the end of the day change and hope and progress it actually just makes me want to vomit.

CLIFF: Need a drink / because six weeks running feels like two years walking.

NEWBIE: I need a drink because my boyfriend left me / for his girlfriend, again, but this time's the last time, until he comes crawling back begging to get crooked till he can't see straight

MIKA: I need a drink cause the last time i had one I don't remember / what happened to me before and after, NO recall

ROBERTA: I need a drink I been dropping dimes /all day for phone lines that never ever pick up

TANO: I need a drink *porque la mierda esta caliente, no trabajo mañana, and my puto landlord puso un raton enormous en mi apartamento.*

A-GAY: I need a drink I need a shot I need a look I need a fuck

PEG: I NEED A DRINK.
…Cause I lost my wallet cause I lost my job cause I got a lost life,
I need a drink
Cause every-time I try to push myself up some prick pushes my back down,
I NEED A DRINK
Because dealing with a life like this sober?
Is beyond over.

...June 27th, 1969, Midnight...

......Jesus fucking *Christ—I / Need. A. Driiiiiiiiiiiiink!*

(Transition)

(Everyone gets ready for the night.)

BAND:
I need a, I need I NEED A DRINK!
I need a, I need I NEED A DRINK!
I need a, I need I NEED A DRINK!
I need a WOOOOOOOOOOOOOOOAH!
I need a, I need I NEED A DRINK!
I need a, I need I NEED A DRINK!
I need a, I need, I NEED A DRINK!
I need a WOOOOOOOOOOOOOOOAH!

NEWBIE:
I need a STIFF-SHOT-SAWED-OFF-ROUGH-RIGHT-
DON'T-THINK
JUST-RIGHT-HARD-TIGHT-RED-LIGHT-BAR-FIGHT
CAN'T-STOP-WON'T-STOP

EVERYONE:
NEW BAR NEXT BLOCK
GIVE IT TO ME LEMME TRY THAT
FATHERFUCKING MOTHERFUCKING-GOD-
DAMN-DRINK!

(They dance)

BAND:
I need a drink!
I need a drink!
I need a drink!

NEWBIE: Stonewall Inn, Midnight, shirts off hard-on big
lights GO!

(The Stonewall Inn)

(We're there, instantly.)

(A big, sweaty, go-for-broke-balls-to-the-walls dance number.)

(NEWBIE controls the energy, and leads everyone through an hour of debauchery in about two and a half minutes.)

(For the first time, we see complete freedom from all the characters—
it's loose, it's sexy, it's fast as fuck and fun as hell.)

(The BAND rocks instrumental punk-power-pop, until the midsection,
which goes like this)

EVERYONE: *(A chant)*
We are the Stonewall Girls, we wear our hair in Curls
We wear our dungarees above our Nelly Knees
We are the Stonewall Girls, We are the Stonewall Girls
Come on and take a whirl you got the Stonewall Girls!

(MIKA and TANO start vogueing as everyone sings.)

(The band builds and builds, and finally we're back to the dance—)

(Everyone moves, especially the ones who can't.)

(Shirts come off, lips get locked, hands, legs, hair, everywhere,)

(And just when things are building to the absolute breaking point—)

COP: *(Enters in full Uniform)*
THIS IS THE POLICE!
WE'RE TAKING THE PLACE!

(The Raid)

(Nobody moves.)

COP: Everybody take out their identification.
Form a line.
You must show identification to leave the bar,

If you resist, You will be arrested.
Anyone resisting arrest, will be brought down by force.

EVERYONE: ....

COP: EVERYBODY! MOVE!

(One by one, they exit. Direct address:)

ROBERTA: The Stonewall Inn

A-GAY: One-thirty A M

MIKA: No air conditioning

TANO: Shirts off

CLIFF & ROBERTA: Alone

COP: Nights OVER, don't make me repeat myself,
MOVE.

EVERYONE: Outside.

(They're gone. Still in D A)

CARSON: ...If you were lucky.

COP: Any men dressed as women or women dressed as
men
Will be interrogated and incarcerated on the spot.
You're dressed
like you're not?
Back bathroom. NOW.

PEG: One forty-five A M

CARSON: That morning

COP: The reports of what happened next are not exactly
clear

PEG: I. WAS. THERE.

(The Bathroom)

(No room to move, completely claustrophobic)

*(CARSON and PEG stand apart, and for the first time in a
long time—silence.)*

CARSON & PEG:

………………
…………
……

CARSON: How was your evening, honey?

PEG: ………………

CARSON: Tough Crowd.

(We hear a police siren, muffled, outside. It's gone.)

CARSON: I had a date tonight.

PEG: —Me too.

CARSON: …Get her number?

PEG: …….

CARSON: Me neither. *(Reaches into his bra)* …You got a wallet on you?

PEG: Got jacked.

CARSON: Nothing to loose then ain't that right?
(He throws his wallet.)
…Ever been inside the pigpen?

PEG: …….

CARSON: Nothing to be scared of. Just make sure /you

PEG: I. **Am Not.** Going to jail. *Tonight.*

CARSON: …That makes two of us.
Any ideas?

CARSON & PEG: ………

PEG: We could switch clothes.

CARSON: …….I could fit in /those pants

PEG: I could wear a dress

CARSON: You'd look good in it

PEG: Take my shoes, /and my shirt

CARSON: Hell, if you can fit into these heels they're *yours* baby, *take* em.

PEG: I could be you.

CARSON: I could be you.

PEG: Think that'd make 'em let us go?

CARSON: Oh, they'd *have to*.
Just a man dressed like a man.
Woman dressed like a woman.
Nothing to see here, "let 'em go through, let 'em out."

PEG: That's what it takes?

CARSON: That's all they want.

CARSON & PEG: …………

PEG: That's a very nice color on you, ma'am.

CARSON: Thank you sir. Thank you very much.

COP: Someone wanna tell me what's going on here?
(He appears.)

(The room turns cold; nobody moves.)

COP: Because.
Either they sent me in a ladies room to find out who the men are…
Or they sent me in a men's room to find out who the ladies are.
So which is which?

CARSON & PEG: ………

COP: …You two are making the game here. I'm just playing by the rules.
Three strikes, you're out.
All-right?
That's *fair*.
You.

CARSON: Evening Officer.

COP: Answer my question.

CARSON: Can you please repeat /yourself

COP: What are you, man or woman, I gotta ask, unless you want me to /search you

CARSON: Well I

COP: *Don't—*
interrupt me.

CARSON: —Yes Officer

COP: Ever

CARSON: Yes Officer

COP: That's *one.*
......So what are you?

CARSON: I'm fucking incredible.

COP: *(Laughs. Breaking the ice)*
—Oh yeah?

CARSON: Yes Officer.

COP: *(Still cracking up)*
Wow, wow-wow!
—You know who I am?

CARSON: —Oh I don't know, Officer.
You all look the same to me.

COP: That's two.
......Tell me what's happening here kid.

CARSON: I'm not a kid. Officer.

COP: So what are you?

CARSON: Isn't it obvious? I'm just a single, hard-working, beer drinking, church-going tax paying full-grown-up-woman and / if

(COP *punches* CARSON *in the gut.)*

COP: ....That's three.
I make no apologies for what comes next *you hear me* I
make no apologies whatsoever for what you make me
do once you've pushed me past my limit,
look-me-in-the-eye, *son.*
NAME.

CARSON: ...Molly Minnelli.

(COP *knocks* CARSON, *nearly across the room.*)

(*He falls to the ground.*)

COP: Stay down.
......Wow.
First time that thing's listened to me.
Good little nigger, stay right there—

PEG: ....

COP: Remember me?
......Arms up, legs out.
I'm not gonna hurt you.
Just need to do a frisk to check you out, protocol, kid.

(PEG *extends her arms.*)

COP: Thank you.
(*He frisks* PEG, *talking to* CARSON.)
Now see, this young man is helping out here,
See what he's doing?
He's being *accommodating.*
He's treating me with respect. He's the—
(*He stops at* PEG's *breast.*
He stays there.)
Oh. Oh no.
This is not good. Oh no.
This isn't supposed to happen.
See. Now. He stopped being accommodating,
(*He goes lower......*)
He stopped treating me with respect,
He stopped trying to make this situation go as

smoothly as possible, no.
(His hands disappear into her pants.
They stay there.)
Close.
No cigar.
......I'm taking you out myself, hear me?
...You *hear me*

CARSON: Get the fuck *off* of him.

COP: Jesus Christ you're a dumb little monkey aren't you?

CARSON: And you're a cock-gobbling-big-headed-peckerwooded-honkey-ass-knuckle-dragging-nose-licking-Father-fucker with no ass no brains and no go damn leg to stand on you shit-eating-cold-hearted-spook.

COP: Gimme your best shot.
It's okay.
You talk a big game, let's see how you play it—
I dare you.
Come on, I'll even give you the first punch, / you
FIGHT.

(PEG stands, still unmoving.)

(CARSON charges—blind, unrestrained, animalistic rage.)

(It's a tight, intense, heavy brawl.)

(CARSON's down. COP grabs him—
rips off his wig.)

COP: ...*That's* all you are, isn't it? *That's* it.

CARSON: ......

COP: The backtalk sass-talk, without the *costume*...
Just another slow-talking overgrown cock-sucking ugly little Nigger.
(He rips the dress.
Down the side, down the front.)

COP: Man you're fucking ugly. God damn man no wonder you cover up.

Fuck did you get this thing, the Five and Dime?

CARSON: *(To* PEG*)* Help /me—

COP: Huh? Didn't hear you Sambo say it again, WHAT?

CARSON: PLEASE. HELP. /ME

*(*COP *knocks* CARSON *to the ground.)*

(He's down.)

COP: …No helping you. Nobody's gonna do that. Know what they're gonna do? They're gonna watch. I'm gonna carry your black ugly mass out there for everyone to see what a god-damn-ugly piece of—

(Suddenly, PEG *pulls* COP'S *gun out of it's holster, and aims it at his face.)*

EVERYONE: ………

COP: Kid? Not the night.

PEG: ………

COP: Not tonight, you don't wanna *try* that tonight.

PEG: …….

COP: You gimme the gun nobody has to know.
Won't say anything.
I'm just gonna take *this one* out—then *you* can leave, behind me, nobody has to know.
Just gonna put him in the wagon take his ass off to jail, you don't have to go, just watch, that's all, so / I'm gonna

PEG: *NO. MORE. WATCHING.*
…Give her back her motherfucking wig.

*(…*COP *does.)*

PEG: Now get on your knees.

COP: ...Please—

PEG: DONE.

Do you hear me? DO YOU / HEAR ME

COP: I hear you

(PEG *advances;*
the gun is inches away from the COP.)

PEG: *Don't interrupt me!* No kids no family no wallet
no money no life I've got nothing to loose you filthy
fatherfucking pig *I-will-take-you-out,* so nobody else
ever has to to lick your shit again *I will take you out.*

COP: PLEASE. Let me just...just one thing—

PEG: ....

COP: Don't take this out on me. Okay? This is *the law.*
I'm just doing what I'm told.
Don't blame me for you being you, okay—
this isn't *personal*—
it's just the way things *are.*
......See? You understand.
Wish the world was different, kid, but it's not—
Not my fault, all right—I'm just a cop.
Gimme. Gimme the gun. Come on, / come on come on
COME ON

CARSON: *Shoothim Shoothim* / **ShoothimGODDAMNIT!**

(*Suddenly,* COP *rushes* PEG,
bending her, grabbing the gun.)

COP: / FREEZE! Stupid little bitch, I SAID FREEZE!

PEG: I wasn't gonna do it / I wasn't gonna do it

COP: (*Calling offstage*) BACKUP, / in here in here we
need BACKUP

PEG: LET-/ ME-GOOOOOOOOOOOOOOOOOOOO!
Let-me-GOOOOOOO!

CARSON: Shoot him, shoot him in the eye *blow his fucking face off* SHOOT HIM!

(Outside Stonewall)

(COP drags PEG outside;)

(The ensemble goes into direct address as COP weaves in between them.)

(PEG doesn't stop screaming. This all happens at once.)

MIKA: Outside / the Stonewall Inn

TANO: One forty-five A M

NEWBIE: 96 Degrees

A-GAY: A hundred people

CLIFF: A hundred people

ROBERTA: Three hundred people
Outside of the Stonewall Inn.
Three hundred people.
Watching.

(The ensemble surround the scene.)

(COP handcuffs PEG as he reads her Miranda Rights.)

COP: *(Sotto Voice)* Move! / MOVE, get out of the way, MOVE!
CALL FOR BACKUP! I repeat, call for backup at the Stonewall Inn on Christopher Street!
"You have the right to remain silent. Anything you say or do can and will be held against you in a court of law. You have the right to speak to an attorney. If you cannot afford an attorney, one will be appointed for you. Do you understand these rights as they have been read to you? Do you? DO YOU?!"

PEG: *NO-MORE-WATCHING!*
You see me scream, you SEE IT,
you don't step, you watch, you stop and watch and wait *till it's your turn,*

your turn to scream, everybody else watches,
waiting for *their* turn to scream and *their* turn to scream
and NO-MORE-WATCHING!
If there's somebody here, if there's somebody here who
can **hear me**, HELP ME,
Somebody do something one-of-you-boys-*stop-this*, do
something, Somebody, SOMEBODY!
NO-MORE-WATCHING!
"We gotta help each other, right?" Right?! Right?!
RIGHT?! RIGHT?!

(COP *bashes* PEG *in the head.*)

(*Once, twice, three times.*)

(*She's done.* COP *picks her up, dragging her out of the scene.*)

(*Thick silence. Nobody moves.*)

(*After a moment,* COP *returns. He stands in front of the ensemble.*)

(*Direct address:*)

(*Last Straw*)

EVERYONE: ....

COP: One fifty-five A M.
June 28th, 1969
96 Degrees
Outside the Stonewall Inn.

ROBERTA: Nowhere to go, nothing to do, nobody to
scream to /yell to call to climb to

CLIFF: Not a god damn camera crew, / newspaper, no
press no nothing

NEWBIE: Nothing to loose anymore

ROBERTA, CLIFF, NEWBIE: NO-MORE- / WATCHING

MIKA: No money, no family, no job, / no life,

TANO: No more beer, no more dancing, /no way out now

ROBERTA: No car, no chance, no law, no rights, nothing to loose anymore, / nothing, nothing, nothing, nothing, nothing not a god-damn-thing-at-all *for the last god damn time.*

COP: …Eight highly trained veteran New York City Police Officers.

ROBERTA: …Three-hundred-and-fifty tired, lost, drunk *angry faggots.*

ENSEMBLE: *(A slow, unleashed avalanche of primal sound.)*
………………*aaaaaaaaaaAAAAAAAAAAAAAAAAAAA*
AAAAAAAAHHHHHHHHHHHH!

COP: Backup, I repeat, we need BACKUP AT THE STONEWALL INN, I REPEAT, BACKUP!

(A Riot)

(The BAND *rocks.)*

(The scene breaks out; lights flashing, bodies pushing, sirens blaring—a relentless clusterfuck.)

(This is not one "scene"; these are remixed bits and pieces; a live, constantly moving slideshow of revolution.)

(Bottles are thrown, garbage cans tossed; debris and destruction spread with wild abandon.)

(Just as soon as it reaches it's climax:)

NEWBIE: Out of the closet and into the streets!
Out of the closet and into the streets!

ENSEMBLE:
OUT OF THE CLOSET AND INTO THE STREETS!
OUT OF THE CLOSET AND INTO THE STREETS!
OUT OF THE CLOSET AND INTO THE STREETS!

COP: *(Direct address)* HOLD!

Reports of what happened next are not exactly clear.

ENSEMBLE: I. WAS. THERE.

(The riot freezes.)

(One by one, the ensemble turns into direct address.)

(They're looking above, beyond. The band builds an approaching, escalating drumbeat.)

TANO: 3 A M.

MIKA: Christopher Street.

ROBERTA: Riot Squad. / Marching

CLIFF: Marching with helmets, / billy clubs

A-GAY: Storm-Shields, walkie-talkies, / marching

NEWBIE: Marching. Marching in perfect time.

ENSEMBLE: *(Eyes to the skies)* ......Tear Gas.

(Tear-gas-pellets shoot from all directions, dropping, instantly filling the stage with smoke.)

(We see the ensemble struggle through the haze, screaming—
the sound-scape intensifies; it's blind calamity.)

(ROBERTA runs to the phone booth for cover. The scene doesn't stop, and through the smoke, we hear)

ROBERTA: Do not retreat! I repeat, do-not-retreat, my brothers and sisters, PUSH-ON, They push back, we push hard,
My brothers and sisters, DO-NOT-RETREAT, REPEAT!

(MADELINE appears through the smoke.)

(ROBERTA is already on the phone.)

(Direct address:)

MADELINE: Street corner, West 10th and 6th Avenue— two blocks AWAY from the insanity.

ROBERTA: Two blocks from The Stonewall Inn, two-fifteen in the morning.

NEWBIE: The Village! Wooooo!
(He rushes across the stage,
totally naked.)
Out of the closets and into the streets! Out of the closets
and into the street!
Out of the closets and into the streets!
(He's gone.)

MADELINE: I Hate. The Village.

ROBERTA: No I won't hold, don'tputmeonhold,
there is something going DOWN on Christopher Street
/ we need the New York Times we need the Daily
News we need every eye in sight because if we lose
this fight we lose the Night, 53 Christopher Street, The
Stonewall Inn, Roberta out, WHAT?!

MADELINE: *(A whisper to a scream)* Excuse me—
Excuse—

Mmm. Hello. Hello. Hello there, my name is Madeline
Walsh,
exc— Stop it, stop it get away from that phone stop it
excuse me hellohello goddamnit speak-to-me!

ROBERTA: —You with *The New York Times*?

MADELINE: I don't give a shit about *The New York
Times*, I don't give a shit about your war, I don't give a
shit about your silly little civil rights all-right I *pretend*
to, *I do,* but I really couldn't rip two shits I DON'T
CARE!
…This is me *nice.*
So, um, "please please pretty pretty fucking please
HELP ME find the Police Department."

ROBERTA: Lady? Get outta my face,
unless you wanna see my fists.

MADELINE: GO TO HELL!

ROBERTA: WE'RE ALREADY THERE!

MADELINE & ROBERTA: ....!

ROBERTA: *(Back on the phone)* Hello this is Roberta /
we need full presence outside of the Stonewall Inn, I
repeat, full presence outside of the Stonewall Inn!

MADELINE: *(Running off)* The police Station! Please,
seventh Precinct police station, SOMEBODY HELP
ME, / HELLO, HELLO!

COP: / Leave the streets!

This is your final warning! LEAVE-THE-STREETS

*(As COP speaks, we get a
super-short-rock transition into:)*

A-GAY: Charles Street. Just beyond the mess.
Brownstone walk-up.
Under the awning. Safe. Untouched.
Three A M.
UNDER THE AWNING

CLIFF: CARSON!
CARSON!

A-GAY: Hey.

CLIFF: Hey, man—hey, /I'm—

A-GAY: You didn't hear me
I said: Hey.
Hey.

CLIFF: Man there's a fucking WAR going on what the
hell / are you doing

A-GAY: Last chance

CLIFF: FUCK you,
CARSON! CARSON!

(TANO runs through.)

TANO: *(Shut the fuck up!)*
"CARSON!" "CARSON!" Who the fuck is Carson,
some long-lost fucking Otter, this is not Gone With the

Wind, papi, you ain't gonna find him, nobody can hear you scream,WALK.

(CLIFF *exits*.)

TANO: …MIKA!
MIIIIIIKA where the fuck are you! MIKA!
You stupid bitch! MIKA!

A-GAY: Hey.

TANO: —Hey.

(TANO *crosses to* A-GAY—)

(*Before he can open his mouth, they kiss*.)

TANO: "My name is Terry Robinson Harley. I live by the deli."

A-GAY: Take my hand.
Shut your mouth.
Follow my lead.
—Is that arrangement acceptable for you?

TANO: —I always wanted this to happen? But —my friend, he's, he's stupid and he needs me and I just tried cocaine for the first time so please,/ please /just help me look—

A-GAY: You're. Begging. Stop.
Let me state the facts.
You're missing your friend, could be the end, but—
It's over.
The cops will make one final sweep, kick everyone out, and then that's it—
nothing more you can do and that's terrible,
but now? You're here with a top.
You're horny, you're hot, and you've wanted me for a long time now.
I'm just stating the facts.
—You have five seconds.
……………Please leave

TANO: I'll see you around—

A-GAY: I don't speak to spics. Wetbacks. Coloreds, whatever you are—you just lost your one.

TANO: …………

A-GAY: Go. Or I'll call the police, they hate you faggots now, don't they?

TANO: I'm not going anywhere.
And I'm not afraid / of the cops anymore—

A-GAY: Let me repeat myself, I SAID GO

TANO: *(The bitch is back and better then ever)*
Because All I see's some skinny-necked pencil-dicked foul-smelling shit-talking-faggot begging me to get his dick licked begging me por meter mano y hechar el polvo, crying *to me* while listen here come mierda nelly bussdown traga leche. I've fucked sailors, doctors, psychics, physicians, truck-divers, ex-attorneys, felons y hasta tu madre cabrona.
I am Tano Rodrigez Santana "Hope" de la Cruz, and I may be a spic. I may be a wetback. I may not even live here, and I don't, okay, I don't live in some shitty little brownstone, okay, but right now I am OUT here. Fighting. Kicking, and screaming, and chanting and running and fighting and screaming *(around and around and around)* and around
—Just so you can stand outside and hitchhike for golden-boys cause you think it's the end and if you're gonna die, you might as well eat out a beef cake before shit blows up, well—
"Look upon me motherfucker.
Behold. A true blue bitch, through and through."
Now Get back inside before I cut you down the middle, through the sides, and throw your cracker-ass in the street, I'll do it, watch me bitch, watch me do it.
…Just stating the facts.

A-GAY: ...Evening.

TANO: GO.

(A-GAY *exits inside.*)

CARSON: You stole my read.

TANO: Ohmygod.

CARSON: Keep it.

TANO: (*What is wrong with you*), ohmygod—

CARSON: (*About to collapse, fight it*)
Stop.
I'm...fine. I'm fine here.

TANO: You need to get inside girl the pigs won't / stop
coming

CARSON: I'm fine.
Let em come.
—I'm waiting for somebody.

(*Transition into police station*)

(*This is all at the same time.*)

MADELINE: / THE POLICE STATION!

ROBERTA: (*On the phone*) / Do not retreat my brothers
and sisters I repeat, do not retreat, REPEAT,
REPEAT, they're coming back now we got more more
shot, one more shot to get this right,
do not retreat, REPEAT!

COP: / LEAVE THE STREETS! ANYONE
FOUND LOITERING WILL BE ARRESTED AND
INCARCERATED ON THE SPOT! LEAVE THE
STREETS!

NEWBIE & ENSEMBLE:
OUT OF THE CLOSETS AND INTO THE STREETS!
OUT OF THE CLOSETS AND INTO THE STREETS!
OUT OF THE CLOSETS AND INTO THE STREETS!

COP: 7th precinct

MADELINE: The police department

PEG: Three forty-five A M
POLICE STATION

(MADELINE *looks up from her chair.*)

(PEG *has just entered the waiting room.*)

(*She looks torn up; black eye, beat-down.*)

MADELINE & PEG: ………………..

MADELINE: …There's something on your face.

PEG: —*No.* Where?

MADELINE: —Well, —your face, there's—
I I I think /you possibly

PEG: Okay.

MADELINE: Do you want me to /get it

PEG: I'm fine

MADELINE: I mean *who knows* where that came from

PEG: Well, I just stepped out of jail.

MADELINE: (*Licks the side of her shirt, approaches*)
—I can get it

PEG: (*Stepping away, wiping her own face*)
Got it—
got it.

MADELINE: —I just don't want you going out in the
street looking like a maniac.

PEG: Too late.

MADELINE & PEG: ……………

PEG: Did I get it?

MADELINE: It's gone.

PEG: Great

MADELINE: Peg

PEG: *Done* here.

MADELINE: Peggy Walsh, *you stop,* right there,
you stand right there and you don't move,
not this time *you stop.*

MADELINE & PEG: ……………..

MADELINE: You look like you're about to faint, you
should sit.

PEG: *(Biggest lie of all time)*
—I'm fine standing.

MADELINE: Peg, you need to go to the hospital

PEG: I didn't ask
for you

MADELINE: But I'm here, / You've *got* me now

PEG: That's not my fault

MADELINE: I came, for you, / I came all the way down
here on the turnpike straight-shot-down-no-stops and
you look at me when I am speaking.

PEG: I don't owe you *anything* by that, not my bag, not
my fault, if I had it my way I'd

MADELINE & PEG: …………

PEG: —If I had it my way I'd still be *inside.*

MADELINE: She wouldn't come.

PEG: …Least inside there I didn't have to deal with
mess.

MADELINE: She called me, she refused / to come down,
to get you

PEG: Do what I want, / say what I want

MADELINE: Oh, Peggy, / we can just go on like this all
night

PEG: *(Stepping to her)* Punch somebody out if they deserved it, I did it, I'd do it again too

MADELINE: Mom doesn't want you anymore.

PEG: *(Totally taken aback)* ......I don't think—

MADELINE: I do, it's true, I know.
For a long time now.
...So she won't come.
She doesn't want you, Peg.
...Look me in the eye.
—I came all this way, and you can't, even look me, in the eye, spoiled little brat, that's *just* like you.
—*I hear things.* You know. The radio, I hear things.
They say its a root issue with your father. I don't know.
I hear things.

PEG: ...You think I'm this way because of Dad?

MADELINE: That's what they said.
Something that—well, I don't know, I just—the radio, I hear things.

PEG: Right.
I'm queer cause my Dad didn't love me.
And that cop over there? He's white cause he ate all his vegetables.

MADELINE: Not the same.

PEG: And you're straight cause ever since you let every Tom Dick and Harry on the street fuck your brains out your cunt's custom cut for cock

(MADELINE slaps PEG.)

MADELINE & PEG: ....

MADELINE: *(Completely honest)* Well, I'm very sorry for that.

PEG: ....

MADELINE: ...When did we loose you Peggy?

PEG: Birth.

MADELINE: Be *honest*.
And don't do it for me, do it for the both of us.
Last time.

PEG: Last time?

MADELINE: ………..

PEG: You *never* lost me.
Never lost me. You *left* me.

MADELINE: …You speak like one of them now.
New Yorkers. You all just / sound the

PEG: Done here?

MADELINE & PEG: ……

MADELINE: Do you need money?

PEG: —Got a job.

MADELINE: —Take some money.
They said you didn't have a wallet when you came in,
which means you don't have a red cent to your name
right now,
I mean it, take a cab, it's late and it's hot and it's New
York and I hear things.

PEG: ……

MADELINE: Ten dollars, take a cab.

PEG: …

MADELINE: Well then *I don't know*, fifty dollars, fifty
dollars, what do you want, will that-
Peg.
I wasn't **meant** to be your sister—
…In the same way.
That you weren't meant to ever, ever, ever marry a
man.
And I, I, I used to think God made a mistake. With *me*.
Because, I could never, ever, *ever*, find it in my heart

to—
Love you, like you loved me, once *I knew*, I could
never, ever look at you the same way again, couldn't.
…But if you—if you could just hold it in?
If you could just—*not do*, what you do,
if you could just be—a woman, if you could do that—
I could *help you*.
You could…I don't know… You could maybe come
back with me in the car.
And we could drive to my house.
And you could meet your niece. *Your niece.*
And you'd have money and a home and a family,
again, and you want that, Peg, I can see it.
Now you're acting tough—and *you're good at it*—but
those bruises… That leg…Peg,
You need medical attention, and I, I, I would be willing
to provide that, for you,
I would be happy to do it.

PEG: …And all I'd have to do—

MADELINE: Is jus*t give this up*. For good.
You wanna see Mom. And me?
And maybe—maybe we could get back to how we
used to be.

PEG: —I have no money.
Bout to lose my apartment.
Fired, last week.
Got nothing.
—And I love you.
I love you *so, so, so* much. Madeline? *I do.*

MADELINE: …Oh, Peggy—

PEG: But I would rather slit my wrists with a dull
straight razor then bury myself ever again for your
favor.

MADELINE: …You won't survive till the end of the year.

PEG: Better dead down here then stuck in hell forever with you.

MADELINE: —Well, I'm, I'm going to my car. Thank you, for this waste of an evening, thank you very much.

PEG: —What's her name?
My Niece?
Please.

MADELINE: …Laura.

PEG: Laura?

MADELINE: Laura. Looks just like you.

PEG: ……Well. In a couple of years. If she turns out just like me?
Just-like-me?
Then what, Madeline. *Then* what.

MADELINE & PEG: …Done.

(End of MADELINE *and* PEG *scene.)*

*(*PEG *collapses into the chair.)*

PEG: …I… Need…a drink.

(The Village)

(4:45 A M)

(Christopher Park)

*(*ROBERTA *on the phone.)*

*(*MIKA *on the stoop.)*

ROBERTA: —Yes, this is Roberta of W-I-L-D, I am calling one more time to tell you to get down to Christopher Park, 55 Christopher Street, right outside the Stonewall Inn, NOW, before it's—

Hello, Hello DO NOT hang up on my ass this is Roberta and I'm on the front lines right now, trying to tell you to wake your ass up and shuffle on down here

there is a DON'T you hang up on me don't you dare
hang GOD damn it.

MIKA: Hey.
It's over ,girl.
Just saw the last pigs up and get down Gay Street.
/*It's over*

ROBERTA: Hello, this is Roberta of W-I-L-D, I need you
to wake up all those ugly dykes at N-O-W tell them
to go to the C-V-O and make some poster board signs
with some T-L-C and head down to the stonewall inn
A-SAP, bring the P and V, /
it's just me it's just ME down here and we can not back
down we back down right now they come back, they
hit us harder, IT'S NEVER EVER OVER
DON'T you DARE hang up I have seen the full extent
of what they can do, to us, tonight, I can see what they
will do, again, tomorrow, I watched,
I watched,
I met a girl tonight.
…And they beat her. Throw her in the back of the
truck.
—And I watched, and you watched, and we all
watched and I don't care if you're tired I'm tired I'm
goddamn tired……
Please… Please.

MIKA: Girl. IT'S OVER. It's done, what, don't just
ignore me come on girl it's OVER with HEY!

(ROBERTA *hangs*.)

MIKA & ROBERTA: ………………………..

ROBERTA: You got ten cents?

MIKA: Girl—

ROBERTA: This
is *all* I can do.

MIKA: …I look like I got ten cents?

(Passes her a bottle.
She sits on the stoop.)

ROBERTA: Thank you my brother.
…What now?

MIKA: Just this.
……Ten o'clock.

ROBERTA: What / about it? Who's ten o'clock what's
ten o'clock—

MIKA: Ten o'clock, coming up on your ten, your ten—
BITCH.

*(*NEWBIE *and* TANO *enter.)*

MIKA: Where in / the hell were you bean queen,
huh, don't, don't snap your hands in my face now
answer me bitch I been waiting for you over here I
THOUGHT YOU WERE DEAD running around like a
bitch without a tit to suck on if you ever do that shit to
me again if you EVER, ever in the history of ever DO
THAT TO ME.

TANO: Oh do / not *(even start with me I have been up*
and down and down and up) and here you are yucking
it up with Angela Davis *(well I've got something to tell*
you honey you are not the last coke in the desert, OK,) I
could have been to the docks, I could have gone to the
bath-house, shit, *(I could have gone home)* YOU STUPID
BITCH.

MIKA & TANO: …………………

MIKA: Got a cigarette?

TANO: I stole a whole pack from when they looted the
deli.

MIKA: Ignorant.

MIKA & TANO: Bitch.
Shit, Jinx, Drink.
(They drink.)

ROBERTA: Mmmhmmm.

MIKA: Girl /Please don't "Mmmhmm" me

TANO: / (*There she goes again*)

ROBERTA: So that's it? You're back and every-thing's the same and every-body's just "snap this" and "bitch that", that's it?

MIKA: ......Look girl, you can keep calling Tom Dick and Henrietta and however.
Or you can see that there ain't nobody around anymore.

ROBERTA: Cause we lost

MIKA: Cause shit's just getting *started*.
...Every day I take two trains. A bus. And a bike to get over here.
To sit on somebody else's stoop.
You ever met the bitches who live up there.

TANO: Hell no

MIKA: I've got no business being here girl, neither does Tano, neither do you.
....But this is where we *live out*, all-right?
So I'm not moving. Not going home today. I'm staying here, and I'm gonna wait.
Cause tonight? Tonight everybody's gonna come back. Trust me.
This shit's just getting started.

NEWBIE: *I'll* be here. I don't have *shit* to do. *Nobody* here has shit to do. It's the fucking summer and it's fucking hot and we're loitering and a couple hours ago I threw a trash can at a cop and last night was the first night in my life I said out loud "I'm Gay" and I didn't run away, I didn't watch, *I stayed*. That's what we do, now, right? No more watching, right?

TANO: We stay.

MIKA: We stay.

ROBERTA: No more watching.

MIKA: *Trust* that, girl. This shit's just getting started.

(Coda)

A-GAY: That night, from my window—
I watched the N Y P D riot squad
take on a street full of people.
I was / there

MADELINE: I was there.
I left. (The Village, horrible place, but—)
I turned on my T V the next night—
Something was—off.

A-GAY: —It didn't end well.
It couldn't have, could it?

MADELINE: Years later? On the radio?
(I hear things,) and on the radio, they were—talking
about the riot

A-GAY: People ask me who started it?
this tall, black, drag queen—
I saw him kick / a cop, that started it, but

MADELINE: There was this story, about a woman who
started the riot.
And for a split second, I thought "That's my Peg".
Oh, but there's no evidence, no true facts, no real way
of knowing

A-GAY: Honestly? It was a Friday night,
and I was pretty blitzed.

MADELINE: It could have been my Peg.
…It was my Peg.

A-GAY: I never went back to the Stonewall Inn again.

MADELINE: That was the last time I ever saw my sister.

(COP *enters the space.*
He weaves through the people.)

COP: On the morning of June 28th, 1969, I helped
facilitate the raid of the Stonewall Inn.
...I don't hate the fags. Never did.
I hate the law being broken and bent backwards till it
snaps, now, the things I did that night?
I feel no remorse for protecting my city from a riot
outside of an illegal bar owned by the Mob.
But every year? On that same night? We get a parade,
we get floats, we get a big fucking party—
for something lacking any Pride, whatsoever.
My Name is Alex McArthur, third generation N Y P D.
I /was there

NEWBIE: I /was there

TANO: I /was there

MIKA: I / was there

(NEWBIE, TANO *and* MIKA *exit as* PEG *enters.*)

PEG: I met a /girl that night

ROBERTA: I met **a girl** that night.

CLIFF: I met a girl /that night.

CARSON: I met /a man that night.

CLIFF: Best god damn night of my life, I'm telling you.

PEG: Somebody told me they saw her the second night
of the riots, yelling, just going to town, screaming
/"Gay Power, Truth on the loose", just going nuts, you
know—

ROBERTA: Gay power, truth on the loose, HOLD me
back now, Ha-ha!

CARSON: My friend told me he saw the fella I was with,
grabbing a bat and beating the /shit out of a cop car,
smashing the shit out of it.

CLIFF: FUCK the pigs, LIBERATE Christoper Street motherfucker, WOOOOOO!

PEG: Some people said they saw her, that same night— surrounded by a group of riot police.
Just kicking the shit out of her. Till she couldn't move.

ROBERTA: We gotta help each other out, right?

CARSON: Said the cops busted him, booked him, shipped him off overseas—
and that was the end of that.

CLIFF: Least I did it my way, before they took me away, right?

(PEG *and* CARSON, *alone.*)

(*Direct address:*)

PEG: …….Me?
I will walk with a limp for the rest of my life / because of what happened in that bar that night.

CARSON: I will walk with a limp for the rest of my life because of what happened in that bar that night.

PEG: Lost my family, /my wallet

CARSON: My dress, my man—

PEG: All for what?

CARSON: For *this.*

CARSON & PEG: ………………

PEG: You do it again? If you had to?

CARSON: —No god damn doubt in my head, honey.

You?

PEG: Over and over. Again and again.

CARSON & PEG: …I was there.

(*The* BAND *comes back to life.*)

MADELINE: 1969: New York City

CARSON: Greenwich / Village

CLIFF: 53 Christopher Street

COP: 1-0-0-1-4

NEWBIE: Middle of the street

ROBERTA: Across from the park

TANO: Sign sticking straight up, / Big letters

A-GAY: Huge sign, impossible to miss

MIKA: Anybody who was anybody met everybody right outside

CARSON: Stonewall.

(The sign flickers to life—Everybody watches—it quickly spurts on, off, on—blackout.)

END OF PLAY